Stocking Stuffer Sex Coupons For Him

dress up night- you pick the outfit

pick something to lick off me

blumpkin (blowjob while taking a shit)

spur of the moment 69 followed by anal

ride me then let me pull out and sperm on face

strap me to bed and ride me

just something that you guys
don't normally do,
but something that you know
he would be into

night out at a strip club
and you both get lap dances

make a sex movie

pegging (if he's interested)

fantasy night
(in which you'd fulfill one of your partner's)

purchase of one toy of his/her choice

position of his/her choice

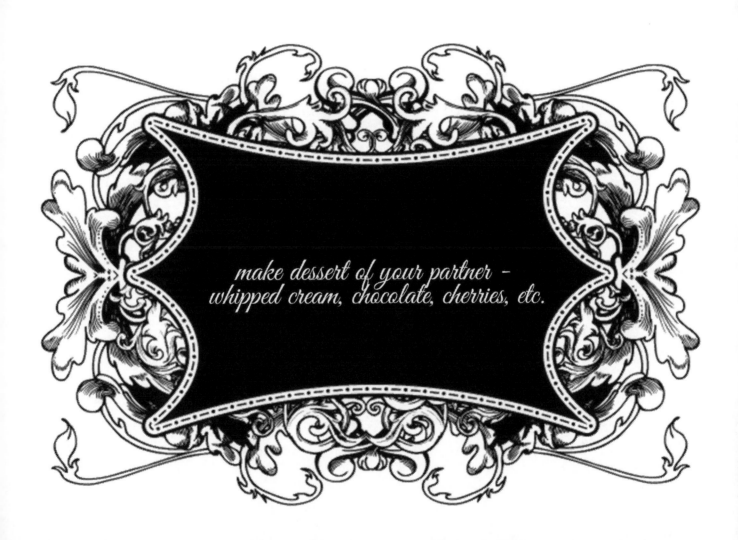

make dessert of your partner –
whipped cream, chocolate, cherries, etc.

fantasy play and naked housework is always good

sexy photo shoot
(if you'd be comfortable with that)

spontanious, random make-outage/sex at the cardholder's whim

anywhere-but-the-bedroom night

*mandantory go to a movie
and make out the whole time night*

strip tease/lap dance

what to wear free pass

do what you want with Ice

whip cream / chocolate syrup

sensual massage followed by blowjob to completion

1 hour oral sex

sex under the stars

licking of choice

bondage - handcuffed/blindfold

one toy of choice

sensual vido rental of choice

XXXmovie night with access
to full participation in whatever

he wishes to do

personal slave service/servan

spanking you/ you being his sex slave for an hour

giving him a blowjob while he is watching porn

serve my favorite meal to me naked